Original title:
The Charm of Lace

Copyright © 2025 Creative Arts Management OÜ
All rights reserved.

Author: Alexander Thornton
ISBN HARDBACK: 978-1-80586-221-5
ISBN PAPERBACK: 978-1-80586-693-0

Threads of Nostalgia Woven

In grandma's trunk, a wild surprise,
Frilly bits and old-fashioned ties.
Stitches and patterns, a tangled mess,
I tried to sew, but made a dress!

Lacework of Forgotten Stories

Once a tablecloth, now a ghost,
It danced with crumbs, we loved it the most.
Torn by a cat, a high-flying leap,
Now it waves goodbye, in grandmama's keep.

Soft Touches of Memory

Dainty edges whispering tales,
Of tea parties, where giggles prevailed.
A mishap involving some jam and a scone,
Now that tablecloth feels all alone!

Footprints on Enchanted Fabric

Each thread a laugh, each hole a cheer,
Mixed up stories of yesteryear.
Remember the time it caught on a chair?
We all fell down, none had a care!

Latticework of Time's Embrace

In a world where patterns tease,
Knots and twists float with ease.
Woven tales from years gone by,
Laughter echoes, oh my, oh my!

Threads of joy in tangled mess,
Funny things we dare confess.
Each stitch holds a silly tale,
A wink, a grin, we will prevail!

Weaving Shadows into Sunlight

Sunlight dances, shadows play,
We knit the darkness into day.
Jokes and giggles, all in threads,
Laughter glows while wisdom spreads.

In the loom, a puppet show,
Twisted yarns, a funny flow.
Sunrise whispers, shadows laugh,
Stitching joy, our silly craft!

Knotting Ages with Gentle Hands

Gentle hands that tie a knot,
Whimsical tales, believe it or not.
Old stories wrapped in yarn so bright,
Each loop a giggle, pure delight.

As ages charm and dance around,
We tie the laughter tightly bound.
Time untangles, with every grin,
In threads of joy, our lives begin!

Dreams Adrift on Lace Wings

Dreams take flight on lacey wings,
Whispers soft, oh what joy it brings.
Floating high with giggles loud,
Embracing silly, it's allowed!

Every twist a spark of cheer,
Adrift in lace, we have no fear.
With every loop a joke unfurls,
Laughter dances, as life twirls!

Anticipation in Every Loop

Tiny threads twist and twine,
Whispers of secrets, quite divine.
I wait for that moment, oh so grand,
When the fabric slips from my hand.

Each stitch holds a giggle, I swear,
A knot tied just for the tear.
Will it hold, or will it flee?
A game of chance, just wait and see!

Fragile Beauty Amongst the Ordinary

Woven lace amidst the clutter,
A mishap waiting, what a flutter!
Pasta stains and coffee drips,
Who knew elegance trips and slips?

A delicate dance in the kitchen's heart,
Why did I think this was smart?
Sift and swirl, I shout with glee,
A napkin's job is not for me!

The Allure of Timeless Textures

Threads entwined like playful cats,
Their quirks and tangles, oh, the spats!
Each loop a riddle, a mistery,
Could it be a scarf or a tapestry?

With patterns bold that sometimes clash,
The fabric giggles, quite the splash.
An olden tale of quirky threads,
We wear our blunders like silly hats!

Dances of Light and Shadow

In bright sunlight, what a sight,
Shadows flutter, quite polite.
They dance across the room with glee,
A lacey jig for you and me!

But when the night falls, what a show,
Ghostly figures, ebb and flow.
An evening's lace with all its quirks,
Who knew a fabric could be such jerks?

A Tapestry of Delicate Echoes

In quiet corners, patterns prance,
A wild frill leads a cheeky dance.
Threads interweave with a giggling breeze,
Laughing lace winks with effortless ease.

A saucy stitch and a playful twist,
Chasing shadows that twist and twist.
A cotton caper, a whimsical sight,
As patterns twirl in faux delight.

Elegance in Every Stitch

Upon the table, chaos resides,
With tangled threads and playful guides.
Each loop a joke, each tie a jest,
In fine designs where fun is best.

A lady's hand with a wink so bright,
Bends the rules in silken flight.
With every pull, a cheeky cheer,
A symphony of giggles near.

Veils of Vintage Romance

A lacey lady, sprightly and spry,
With frills that flutter as she zooms by.
Her vintage flair, a jester's hat,
Spreading joy with each feathered spat.

Romance is silly, a light-hearted foe,
With tangled dreams in a patch of glow.
Stitching smiles in a comical trance,
As ribbons twirl in a silly dance.

Shadows of Graceful Filigree

In shadows deep, where whispers play,
A cheeky lace finds reasons to sway.
With every twirl, a shadow's delight,
Crafting chuckles through day and night.

Lace frolics about like a lively sprite,
Casting giggles in morning light.
A filigree of frolicsome art,
Where laughter and fabric never part.

Timeless Filigree

In tiny threads, a secret waits,
A playful dance, weaving fates.
With nimble fingers, chaos unwound,
A fabric of folly, joy is found.

The cat leaps high, a pounce so fine,
Tangled in yard, oh what a line!
He thinks he's chic, a fashion star,
But he's just lace on a whimsical bar.

A Tapestry Unfurled

Colors clash in a joyful spree,
Creating chaos, all for free.
Thread getting caught in a napping shoe,
What's a grand quilt without a boo?

The grandma laughs, she can't take it back,
Her masterpiece turns into a snack!
With stitches gone wild, it's a sight to see,
A hilarity quilt made by a bee.

Veils of Mystery

In shadows deep, a veil draws near,
Hiding the mess, oh so dear.
A tip-toeing dog, with grandeur and grace,
Did he just trip on a lace place?

Secrets fly like feathers in air,
Behind the drapes, there's laughter to share.
A ghost in a frill, does a jig in the night,
Who knew lace could give such a fright?

Softly Stitched Remembrance

Every stitch holds a tale so sweet,
Of laughter and blunders on nimble feet.
Nostalgia whispers, oh what a scene,
The time when grandma crafted a queen.

Oh, but a sneeze sent the thread a-flying,
The crown got tangled; oh, how they were crying!
A regal mess, what a glorious sight,
A royal affair became a kite flight!

Echoes in Fragility

Delicate whispers, threads that sway,
A cat pounces, foils the ballet.
Patterns that tangle, what a delight,
Giggles erupt, all through the night.

Floating like feathers in the breeze,
Caught up in corners, they aim to please.
An accidental twist, a moment to sigh,
Looming mishaps, oh my, oh my!

Filaments of Beauty

Strings of laughter, tangled in fun,
Grandma's creation? Not quite the one!
A swirl, a twirl, they flutter and flop,
Knots that resemble a shopping cart stop.

Each loop and bow, a wobbly mess,
Dancing with grace, more or less.
A honeycomb pattern, sweet as can be,
Oh dear, there's a sock stuck—who threw that at me?

The Dance of Threads

Threads in a conga, moving in time,
Mismatched and quirky, an odd little rhyme.
The lace takes a bow, but oh! It gets stuck,
The couch is a runway, how'd we get so mucked?

With a skip and a hop, they frolic along,
A batty parade where nothing feels wrong.
Fingers in chaos, we laugh and we play,
Unraveling stitches, come join in the fray!

Lacework of the Heart

A heart made of fibers, what will it say?
It giggles and jigs in a cheerful ballet.
Love's polka dots tangled, a quirky embrace,
Reminds us of moments that quicken the pace.

Each knot tells a story, quite silly and bright,
Of late-night confessions and pillow fight nights.
So nod to the chaos in threads that unite,
For laughter unravels and makes the day right.

Enchantment in Every Handmade Flourish

Threads dance in a merry twist,
Stitches prance like a cheeky lisp.
Each knot a giggle, every loop a jest,
Crafted with love, a playful quest.

Cups of tea spill on a fine lace dream,
Invisible fairies plot and scheme.
With needle and thread, they weave their wit,
In a world of yarn, nothing is quite fit.

Laid Bare by the Fingers of Time

Old lace whispers secrets of yore,
As dust bunnies giggle at the floor.
Time's tick-tock on a fragile base,
Finds wrinkles that chuckle, a funny face.

Stitched stories unravel in a dance,
Each pattern a riddle, a chance romance.
A twist here, a turn there, life's little joke,
Weaving old tales from the wisps of smoke.

Swaying to a Whispering Tune

A breeze waltzes through the lacey frill,
Each flutter a laugh, a giddy thrill.
Curtains sway like dancers in glee,
As sunlight tickles with glimmering spree.

The world's a stage, lace drapes the show,
With actors in ruffles, putting on a glow.
They bow with glee, in patterns so spry,
Chasing giggles beneath a blue sky.

The Language of Woven Wishes

In a thread of dreams, wishes stitch tight,
Crafting a giggle, a twinkling light.
With every loop, hope takes a seat,
In this fanciful dance, nothing's discreet.

The fabric hums a whimsical tune,
As wishes flutter like a merry balloon.
Each small creation, a tale it does tell,
In the land of make-believe, all is well.

The Warmth of Gentle Threads

In a world where fibers play,
Threads giggle as they sway.
Dancing needles, what a sight,
Stitching dreams from day to night.

A tangled mess? Oh, what a show!
Knots and loops put on a glow.
Passing scissors, hear them snicker,
These playful threads just want to flicker.

Each tiny stitch, a joke to tell,
Embroidered puns, all is well.
With every knot, a little tease,
Who knew crafting could bring such ease?

At the end of all this fun,
We gather 'round, our work well done.
With laughter we'll adorn the cloth,
A masterpiece we'll proudly froth.

Filigree Fables and Fabric Fantasies

Once upon a thread so fine,
Fabric critters danced in line.
Twisting, turning, what a prance,
This fable spun from yarns of chance.

In stitches bold, a tale unfolds,
Whiskers twitch, and laughter molds.
Patchwork pals with silly hats,
Woven tales and chippy bats.

A fabric fox sings a tune,
Counting sheep beneath the moon.
Each tiny weave a quirky note,
Sailing on this fabric boat.

As fibers giggle and fabric sways,
Magic happens in playful ways.
Weaving tales with every turn,
In our quilts, we now discern.

Stitches of Heartfelt Hopes

With every stitch, a wish we mend,
Hearts in fibers twist and bend.
Sewing up laughter with a smile,
Making memories all the while.

Silly patches on a frown,
Dancing lightly, no falling down.
Hopeful threads woven tight and bright,
Playful dreams in colors that excite.

An artist's hand, a joyful dance,
The fabric sings, inviting chance.
With every tug and every pull,
Stitches swirl, creating a lull.

So gather 'round, let's weave anew,
With silly tales and threads so blue.
In laughter stitched, our hearts ignite,
Making magic through the night.

The Enchantment of Fragile Patterns

A tapestry of giggles spun,
Fragile patterns join the fun.
Dainty loops, a lightweight song,
Carried along, it can't go wrong.

Patterns prance like butterflies,
In a quilt of whimsical size.
Each design claims a charmed space,
Tickling hearts in this soft embrace.

With threads that twirl and curves that sway,
Every piece has something to say.
Laughter weaves through every seam,
In fragile patterns, we find our dream.

So here we go, let's sew with glee,
Creating wonders—come stitch with me!
In a world where fabric takes flight,
Magic happens, oh so bright!

Delicate Whispers of Feminine Grace

In the attic, threads unwind,
A tangled mess, oh how refined!
Grandma's secrets, oh what a sight,
Kittens play in fabric delight.

Lacy edges tease the breeze,
A game of peek-a-boo with ease.
Could they be armor, or just for fun?
A frilly crown, for everyone!

When I wear it, do I sway?
Or just trip and fall, hooray!
Patterns dance, a playful race,
Who knew fabric could embrace?

Whispers soft, but jokes abound,
Lace can lift you off the ground.
In every stitch, a grin appears,
Fashion's folly, bring the cheers!

Woven Paths of Hope and Desire

Threads of gold, oh what a find,
Tangled hopes, all intertwined.
Each knot a laugh, each loop a sigh,
Weaving dreams that float and fly.

With each pattern, a tale unfurls,
Of silly dances and twirling girls.
A fabric maze, who shall we chase?
Tickled pink, in this wild space.

Hope's a stitch, that pulls so tight,
In every bobble, a joke takes flight.
Wishing for grace, while tripping low,
In lace we trust, go with the flow.

Threads of whimsy in colors bright,
A fabric party, what a sight!
Joyfully sewn, with comic flair,
Woven paths lead us everywhere!

Interwoven Journeys in Soft Light

In soft light, the laces tease,
A wobbly path, oh what a breeze!
Watch your step, or lose your shoe,
Over these laces, who knew?

Lace and laughs, a wild affair,
Catching sunlight in the air.
Each twist a giggle, each turn a grin,
A playful chase, let's begin!

Journey through patterns, tender and sweet,
Avoiding puddles with comic feat.
Over the bumps and under the sun,
In soft stitched laughter, we all run.

With every stitch, a story told,
Of tangled days and hearts so bold.
As we wander, playful and light,
In soft embrace, we find our flight!

A Cascade of Stitched Dreams

A cascade falls, with laughter bright,
Dresses twirl, what a sight!
Laces flying, oh what fun,
In this patchwork race, we run.

Stitches whisper, "Let's not be plain,"
Catching colors in our train.
Life's a tapestry, so sublime,
We laugh and stitch, in our prime.

Adventures sewn with every thread,
Dodging pillows, that's the spread.
Which way to twirl? Oh dear me!
A fabric festival, wild and free!

In a world of lace, so dear,
Every stumble draws us near.
With a wink and a twinkling seam,
Wrapped in laughter, we all dream!

Woven Whispers Under Moonlight

In shadows where the patterns dance,
A spider spins, given the chance.
Her web, a fabric of giggles and sighs,
Tickles the night as the moonlight climbs.

The critters gather, a frisky crew,
Picking out threads of silver and blue.
With every twist, they laugh and twirl,
In a lacey land, where mischief unfurls.

Each loop a secret, each knot a jest,
A playful weave that's simply the best.
As starlight falls on their frolicsome spree,
The night wears its fabric, wild and carefree.

Echoing Elegance Through Generations

Grandma's table, a sight to behold,
With lace like stories we once were told.
It flutters like gossip, with patterns so bold,
Whispering tales of both young and old.

A teacup shivers, a saucer runs wild,
Each stitch a memory of times reconciled.
Oh, the laughter that blooms in spun threads divine,
Making our days so splendidly fine.

The cats love to tumble, they think it's their game,
Chasing the edges, oh what a shame!
Yet still Grandma chuckles, with joy on her face,
Even if somehow, they tore up her lace.

Loveliness in Each Woven Twist

Twists and turns, oh what a delight,
A lace's lollipop, sugary and light.
A swirl with a giggle, a roll with a laugh,
Who knew a fabric could be such a craft?

Stitches like secrets, fold after fold,
With laughter so bold, and stories retold.
A fashion faux pas or a daring surprise,
All in good humor with sparkly eyes.

When all is said, do we really care,
If the lace drapes right or floats in the air?
For joy is the fabric that we all need,
And a good pun to lighten the creed.

Secrets Stitched in Scarlet

A seamstress giggles with mischief in mind,
Stitching red hearts where some should unwind.
Each little secret, a pinch of romance,
With lacy layers that wiggle and dance.

Oh, darling, don't fret if a thread should unlace,
It's merely a chance for a silly embrace.
A snicker, a wink, and a playful spin,
For laughter works wonders when you're in a grin.

When life becomes tangled, embrace the bizarre,
In dreams spun of fabric and voices from afar.
For the secrets in stitches can always unwind,
Bringing joy to the heart, forever entwined.

The Lattice of Stories Unfolding

In a world so fine and neat,
Threaded tales with playful feet.
A dance of knots, a twisty ride,
Where secrets in the folds reside.

Laughter loops through every seam,
Every thread a quirky dream.
Stitches talk with cheeky grins,
As fabric spins the yarn of sins.

With patterns bright and colors bold,
Adventures waiting to be told.
Each lacey strand a tease in play,
Woven whims that dance and sway.

So let us dive in twinkling spins,
In this act, true fun begins.
With every thread and every hue,
Life's a fabric made for two.

Patterns in the Quiet Moments

In the hush where whispers hide,
Pockets full of jokes and pride.
Laughter sprinkles through the grain,
Patterns form 'neath joy and pain.

A lacy print tells of the day,
Folly sewn in every sway.
Like butterflies in silly flight,
Dancing through the threads of night.

Silly shapes all intertwined,
Witty knots that fate designed.
Each loop a laugh, each twist a cheer,
Echoes of the past draw near.

In these moments, remnants cling,
With lace, let joy be our king.
In the quiet, life is spun,
Woven tales of laughter run.

Embraces Woven in Intrigue

Stitched with giggles, hugs untold,
Wrap me tight, let warmth unfold.
In each loop, a surprise awaits,
As friendships weave through open gates.

A lace-bound plot begins to bloom,
In cozy corners, chasing gloom.
Every twist unveils a grin,
Embraces soft as gentle skin.

Fingers play like they know best,
Creating patterns for the jest.
In tangled threads, we find our way,
To silly games where we must stay.

So come, let's spin this yarn once more,
With laughter echoing to the core.
In these bindings, hearts enclose,
A tapestry that always glows.

Fleeting Touches on Gentle Fabric

A fleeting whisper, a tickled lace,
Almost hidden in the space.
Where stitches flirt with every chance,
A lighthearted fabric dance.

With every touch, a story's spun,
Twirling threads for only fun.
Patterns peek and playfully tease,
As laughter drifts upon the breeze.

Like playful pets in soft embrace,
Woven whims take up their place.
On gentle fabric, joys ignite,
Fleeting touches bring delight.

So let's enjoy this silken spree,
In fabric's quilt, just you and me.
With every stitch, we laugh and sing,
In this world, let joy take wing.

Twisted Elegance

In a garden of frilly chaos,
Dresses dance while skirts toss.
A twirl reveals a hidden lace,
A cat chases threads at wild pace.

Tiny fingers try to unwind,
With laughter echoing, hearts aligned.
What a sight, both fun and fair,
Who knew fashion has this flair!

Patterns swirl like cotton candy,
Making grandma feel quite dandy.
Watch out, the boys might swoop and dive,
In this lace trap, who will survive?

A clumsy stumble, oh what a bang!
As lace gets tangled, laughter sang.
In the midst of frivolous fight,
Twisted elegance takes flight!

Whispers of Woven Threads

Threads that giggle in the breeze,
Tangled tales among the trees.
A squirrel wearing lace so bright,
Hops about, what a sight!

Dancing 'round in mismatched shoes,
Leaves rustle with silly news.
A picnic blanket, full of holes,
As ants parade, in it's their goals.

A playful tug, and off it goes,
Laughter brightens our little woes.
Each woven whisper holds a jest,
As friends all gather, feeling blessed.

A bonnet made from frilly scraps,
Turns heads with giggles, and a few claps.
Woven tales that make us cheer,
In this chaos, joy is near!

Gossamer Dreams in Twilight

In twilight's glow, a party gleams,
With gossamer and chocolate creams.
A ghost in lace does take a snack,
As friends all giggle, never lack.

Swirling skirts like cotton fluff,
Boys in bowties looking tough.
Wrapped in lace, they dance and slide,
Chasing shadows, full of pride.

Out comes a whisper, a playful tease,
As lace gets caught among the trees.
With every laugh, the night grows bright,
What a splendid, funny sight!

A lacey joke to share with all,
As giggles turn into a brawl.
Under moonlit, fabrics twirl,
In this dream, laughter unfurl.

Intricate Patterns of the Heart

In patterns spun with joy and grace,
A quilt of smiles lights up the space.
What a puzzle, all askew,
Each stitch laughs, just like you!

Hearts are tangled, oh so sweet,
In lace that dances on our feet.
With boisterous cheer, we spin around,
In this merry, crazy ground.

A friendship patch, all out of rhyme,
We wear our humor like a crime.
Oh look! A lace gone rogue, it seems,
In this chaos, we weave our dreams!

Patterns shout with colors bright,
Laughter echoes through the night.
With every twist, we play our part,
In these intricate patterns of the heart.

Delicate Whispers

Tiny loops and swirls so bright,
A spider's dance in morning light.
I wore it once, to quite a fuss,
My cat took off, oh what a bus!

When friends all gather near the table,
They laugh at me, I hardly able.
My lace was caught, it snagged a cake,
A dessert disaster, what a mistake!

Slipping through fingers like a breeze,
I tried to fix it, if you please.
But it unraveled, oh dear me,
A fashion statement, wild and free!

So now I wear it with a grin,
For who knows where the fun begins?
In every thread, a story speaks,
Of laughter shared for many weeks.

Threads of Elegance

A curtain sways in playful jig,
With lace that plays a game so big.
It whispers tales with every breeze,
I trip on it while trying to tease!

At Sunday brunch, my friends all smirk,
Each napkin folded like a work.
But one sly glance and zoom it goes,
My drink spills out, oh how it flows!

A toddler runs, a chase ensues,
The lace is caught in little shoes.
They giggle loud, as I turn red,
My fancy dinner dreams are dead!

Yet still I wear it, bold and clear,
For laughter's worth more than a sneer.
In every stitch, there's joy to find,
A ruffled charm, oh one of a kind!

Tangles of Time

In grandma's chest, old lace awaits,
It's seen some parties, laughs, and dates.
But tangled now like a wild vine,
I pull one thread, and oh divine!

My cat jumps in, thinks it's a game,
With every leap, there's lace to blame.
She rolls and spins, a tangled mess,
A feline fashion, I confess!

Trying to fix this grand old cloth,
I trip again, but that's my troth.
With every tug, it grows and grows,
A make-shift scarf, despite my woes!

Yet when I wear it, heads do turn,
For laughter's glow, I surely yearn.
In every knot, a tale we weave,
A legacy that we believe!

Gossamer Dreams

The curtains flutter, a soft ballet,
In fancy lace, I lose my way.
Dancing round with friends in glee,
They trip on seams as they agree!

A pirate's prize, the lacy catch,
With every twist, we laugh and hatch.
"Ahoy!" they shout, and off we go,
Lace discovered, putting on a show!

But alas, it snags on every chair,
With every move, I'm just laid bare.
A wardrobe faux pas, they all declare,
Yet in my heart, I just don't care!

For every snag, each silly slip,
Adds to the joy, a merry trip.
In gossamer dreams, we romp and play,
With laughter leading the way!

A Stitch in Enchantment

In a room where threads entwine,
A cat sneezes, oh what a line!
A needle darts with playful glee,
While fabric giggles, just wait and see.

A twirl of lace, sparks start to fly,
Grandma watches, with a twinkling eye.
"Don't pull that thread!" she warns with flair,
But who can resist this wild hair?

Buttons dancing, oh what a sight,
Stitching up dreams in the bright moonlight.
With every loop and every swish,
A fashion faux pas, oh what a wish!

So grab your yarn, don't be a bore,
Create something wacky, oh, we want more!
Let laughter weave through every seam,
In this fine thread, let's live the dream!

Hued Connections

Colors clash in a riotous spree,
Pink and polka dots? Who would agree?
A scarf goes missing, what a surprise,
It's tangled in socks, right by your eyes!

A patchwork quilt with mismatched spots,
Each stitch a story of woeful knots.
My dog wears a hat, so very bright,
Who knew he'd strut with such delight?

In every snip, there's laughter and cheer,
With each odd patch, our friendship's clear.
For in this mess of colorful glee,
We find connections in fabric's spree!

So grab your markers, let's go amiss,
Designs so silly, who knows what bliss?
A tapestry of humor, let's unite,
In a world of fabric, laughter takes flight!

Ribbons of Memory

A ribbon fell, oh where'd it go?
Lurking in pockets, claiming the show.
Tied to a chair, with a twist and a bend,
Each twist a giggle, around the next friend!

Memories dangle from bows gone wild,
A corsage mishap, oh, who's that child?
Waving so proudly, in a gown too bright,
She spun in circles, joy took flight!

With every hue, a tale unfolds,
Of socks worn two ways, oh, how bold!
A garland hangs from the ceiling high,
"Is that a bird?" oh my, oh my!

So weave those ribbons, tie them tight,
In this fun chaos, there's sheer delight.
For life's a party, a colorful fest,
In the ribbons of memory, we're truly blessed!

Wanderings in Whimsy

Oh, where's that button, it rolled away?
On a trip to the couch, where shadows play.
Under cushions, it finds its crew,
A mismatched brigade, so wacky and true.

Shirts that dance in the laundry's spin,
Twirl on the floor, let the fun begin!
Socks that disappear, the great sock thief,
In this fabric race, we find our relief!

With every snip, adventure ignites,
A cape for the cat, he's ready for flights.
"Just one more stitch," we giggle and sigh,
As patches tumble, oh look, they fly!

So let's wander in whimsy, free as the breeze,
Creating outfits that rattle and tease.
For in this journey of thread and lace,
Life's a fun carnival, join the embrace!

Ethereal Patterns of the Past

Once on a dress, a ghost did prance,
With threads so fine, they twirled in dance.
Each stitch a story, each knot a tale,
Whispers of laughter in each frilly veil.

Dresses with secrets, they laugh and tease,
Caught in the cupboard, blowing in the breeze.
Stuck in a loop, a lace-trimmed loop,
Even the fabric is part of the troupe.

Colors like rainbows, but one shade of gray,
Said, 'I'm a bowtie for a cat on play!'
What fun for a tea party, a high-flying vest,
Even the chairs wear their best, not the rest.

In the attic, the lace speaks in curvy sense,
Debating if frills are really that dense.
A tussle unfolds, who wins is unclear,
But everyone bursts out in raucous cheer!

Moments Captured in Fine Thread

Stitches and giggles fit snugly in seams,
Sewn into dreams with whimsical beams.
Buttons retreat, afraid of the chat,
While lace promised laughter—imagine that!

A fabric of moments, a quilt of delight,
Each thread is a story, both silly and bright.
Worn by a fairy who dances at night,
Beneath a full moon, by twinkling starlight.

Patterns like puzzles, they twist and they fold,
Tales of lost kittens and yarn balls of gold.
A mischief of stitches, they weave and they spin,
With laughter so hearty, you can't help but grin!

Caught in a tangle, a yarn goes astray,
While needles and bobbins engage in ballet.
Moments captured, not missing a stitch,
Creating a ruckus, they cause quite a glitch!

Delicate Bonds and Tender Ties

A knot here, a bow there, life's such a race,
We're tied up in laughter, a lace-covered space.
Friends all woven, with glittering seams,
Stitching together our wildest dreams.

Stringing up smiles in the quirkiest way,
Bobbling with joy that won't fade away.
Laces like fairies with twinkling embraces,
Dancing in sunlight, each puff of their paces.

Glitches in knitting, a twist and a twirl,
A tangled-up scarf could make quite the whirl.
Swapping our tales with audacious flair,
Even if one finds a snare in her hair!

Life threads together, with bobbins galore,
Cackles and giggles from each open door.
So raise a fine toast with decorative cups,
For friendship is tangled and never gives up!

Lace and Lullabies of Longing

A song of the laces, a lullaby spun,
By grandmas and fairies, oh, so much fun!
Tickling our dreams with soft whispers of thread,
Hoping for kisses and crumbs in our bed.

While lace whispers stories from times long ago,
Of playful little kittens that stole every show.
The moon in the corner, a winking delight,
Swings in the shadows dance through the night!

With bows in their tails and hearts of pure glee,
The lace keeps on chatting as wild as can be.
'Let's wrap up together and twirl 'round the room,
Looking for mischief, let's cast out the gloom!'

So come, little child, bring your dreams to the lace,
For giggles and wonders can never erase.
Each stitch an adventure, each pattern a whim,
Lullabies echo with giggles and brim!

Gentle Traces

In the drawer, a fabric delight,
A tangle of edges greets the night.
Beneath the dust, it giggles and teases,
On my hand it twists, as it pleases.

A cat on the table, with paws all a-flair,
Tangles that treasure, caught in her hair.
I try to untangle, she purrs in delight,
Doesn't even notice that it's quite a sight.

A ghostly old napkin with patterns so fine,
Whispers of tea spills and a history divine.
Each stitch a secret, each thread a song,
In the hands of a clumsy, it won't last long.

But oh, how it dances, this wonderful lace,
With its knotted adventures, it's hard to keep pace.
I wear it with laughter, though it drags on the floor,
A joyful misfit, who needs something more!

The Art of Subtlety

A ladle and spoon, they waltz in the air,
With lace in the mix—well, it's hardly fair!
The cakes take a tumble, the cream takes a dive,
It's a baking disaster, but oh, we're alive!

My apron adorned with a filigree frown,
Each sprinkle and swizzle, it's chaos in town.
When frosting begins to resemble a blob,
I pretend I'm an artist, my skills I do lob.

The lace on the table, too pretty to mind,
Still watching the show, we joke, "What a find!"
It catches the butter and perhaps some hot tea,
A party of stains—how costly it could be!

Yet laughter erupts as we slice up the pie,
The lace napkin giggles, "Oh me, oh my!"
It captures the crumbs of our culinary jest,
As friends, we declare, lace always knows best!

Whimsical Weavings

In a shop of laces, a mischief I found,
A roll that rolled over, just playing around.
It tangled with ribbons, they danced on the floor,
A whimsical party, who knows what's in store?

A parrot named Larry, he swoops in, and squawks,
He wears my creations, and struts like he rocks.
With a lacey sombrero, he's quite the charmer,
I swear he could cook a Spanish fiesta in armor!

We dip into thrift shops, collect all the stash,
Old doilies and fragments that make quite the splash.
With twirls and with swirls, our laughter does soar,
As we patch together what life has in store.

Oh, the joy in the mayhem, the colors, the flair,
Each piece tells a story, beyond what they wear.
With knotted ideas that sparkle and dance,
In this ludicrous tapestry, we find our romance!

Lacebound Journeys

Packed for a trip with a lace around my hat,
With a wink to the customs, "What's wrong with that?"
As the plane takes off, I sip on my tea,
While my lace is also flying—you should see!

It flutters and wiggles, spilling all my snacks,
Causing giggles from strangers, their colorful hacks.
A lacey persona, it steals the show,
My lunch has a style, don't you think so?

At the beach, it drapes over sandcastles proud,
Perhaps adding flair, to the most lovely crowd.
With sunblock and waves, it twirls like a queen,
Though a crab takes a dash, with a serious glean.

But all of my mischief, I wear with a grin,
In this voyage of laughter, let the chaos begin!
For every adventure that I undergo,
It's laced with good humor, and always aglow!

Fluttering Memories Among Threads

In a drawer, they dance and play,
Little patterns from yesterday.
Twists and knots, a tangled spree,
Lace giggles softly, just wait and see.

Once I wore them, felt like a queen,
Got stuck on a fence, oh what a scene!
With flair, I stumbled, oh what a sight,
Lace leaves me laughing, what a delight!

Giggles echo, as I recall,
Flimsy threads, they started it all.
A sticky donut, oh how I grinned,
Lace on my head, like a win for the win!

So many memories, woven so neat,
Some with mischief, oh what a feat!
With every flutter, I find a chuckle,
In lace we trust, oh let's not shuffle!

Invisible Threads of Connection

In a cafe, I spilled my drink,
Lace napkin saved me, what do you think?
It whispered secrets, holding too tight,
Stains on my shirt, oh what a sight!

My grandma's lace, it's got some flair,
Every stitch a tale, I swear!
Each tiny loop, a hug so sweet,
Invisible threads pull us to our feet!

At dinners, it served like a classic play,
Twirled around like it was ballet.
A slip of the hand, a fork took flight,
A lace rescue, it saved the night!

When I wear it, I can't help but twirl,
Laughing at life, it makes me whirl.
Oh lace, my sidekick, you've got my back,
Even when I trip, you're on the track!

Lace and the Language of Love

A heart shaped doily, spices the air,
Declares my affection, beyond compare.
Every little hole, a whisper so fine,
"Love me like this, and we'll be divine!"

Dinner by candlelight, lace on the table,
Until the cat pounced, quick like a fable.
It flew with a flourish, oh what a scene,
Dinner was chaos, like a funny meme!

In love's embrace, with lace so bold,
Every stitch, a story untold.
I made a heart banner, to woo my sweet,
But the lace fell down like it couldn't compete!

Each tangled thread, a tale of its own,
Crafting emotions, easily shown.
In this fabric dance, we find our way,
With laughs and laces, we'll always stay!

Threads of Dreams and Desires

In a dream, I wore lace shoes,
Dancing with kittens, oh what a muse!
They twirled around, with nimble paws,
While lace still giggled, a slight, sly cause.

Wish upon threads that twist and gleam,
Taking me places, oh what a dream!
In a box of luck, lace held the key,
Unlocking giggles, just wait and see!

With each tiny knot, a wish takes flight,
Filling the air with dreams so bright.
In this merry dance, lace leads the way,
While each little fray tells me to play!

So let's weave the dreams, with some flair,
Dancing through life without a care.
With lace in our hearts, we laugh and twirl,
Threads of delight in this whimsical whirl!

Threads of Time and Tenderness

In a world of twirls and frills,
Threads weave tales like silly drills.
A grandmas' secret from long ago,
Doilies rank high in the show,

Under the table, a cat lies still,
Pawing at threads with a sly little thrill.
While we sip tea, with crumbs on our face,
We giggle and plot a lace-wrapped chase.

The clock ticks loudly, yet we forget,
Time dances wildly; not a worry or fret.
In patterns so fine and sentiments bold,
Our laughter weaves warmth, a sight to behold.

Dances of Lace in the Breeze

Lace socks flapping on wiggly feet,
I tripped on the hem, oh what a feat!
The wind takes a jumper for a wild spin,
While I fumble and laugh, oh where do I begin?

A polka-dot dress tags along in jest,
As we twirl and tumble, I feel so blessed.
Life's little hiccups with fabrics so fine,
Provide giggles and fun in this grand design.

Chasing visions of dreams and of fun,
Each patchwork of laughter has just begun.
With patterns that flutter and sway in the breeze,
We splash through the puddles like kids at ease.

Intricacies of Love's Embroidery

Threading through laughter, heart and stitch,
Every tiny knot is a loveable glitch.
A weave here, a loop there, precision so rare,
Just like my dance moves—beyond compare!

With a needle of joy, we poke and prod,
Creating a quilt that even gods applaud.
Each quaint little misstep, a lumpy delight,
We chuckle and patch with pure delight.

Stitches that spark joy in every design,
Whispering secrets, both yours and mine.
As we thread through this life, let's take care,
To embroider it gold, with laughter to share.

Lace Skirts and Wishes Untold

A skirt made of whispers, lace spun with dreams,
Hiccups of laughter, oh how it gleams.
With every twirl, the wishes take flight,
Around and around, we dance through the night.

My best friend's dress is a sight to behold,
A walking mishap, both funny and bold.
As we trip over teacups and laugh till we cry,
We weave tales of joy that never say die.

Wishes are tangled in all of this flair,
Crashed parties, fun moments, all hanging in air.
In a world full of fabric, we'll dance till we fall,
Embroidered with giggles, our best suit of all.

Charms in the Weaving of Life

In a world of ribbony threads,
A grandmother crochets with grace,
Her cat jumps, a pounce on my head,
Now I'm sporting a woolly embrace.

Dancing patterns in silly loops,
Knots bring giggles, tangled woe,
Life's a quilt of funny groups,
One too many yarns, oh no!

Every stitch is a chuckle shared,
My dog thinks it's his brand new toy,
As tangled threads, we are ensnared,
Laughter bursts; oh what a joy!

So here's to laughter flat and round,
In the coils where chaos meets glee,
In the weaving, magic is found,
Life's fabric: a wild jubilee!

A Symphony of Delicate Veils

A curtain flutters, a ghostly dance,
I trip on ruffles, whoa, oh dear!
The cat thinks I've a clumsy chance,
To play hide and seek with sweet cheer.

Whiskers tangled in gauzy grace,
They map out a labyrinth of fun,
Each flutter, a giggling embrace,
While I fumble 'til day is done.

My friend drapes a veil as a cape,
Proclaiming herself the queen of fads,
In her grandeur, there's no escape,
From laughter that springs from our jags.

So here's to laughter, stitched on light,
In the symphony of fabric's sweep,
With giggles echoing through the night,
Our woven tales make our hearts leap!

Softly Spun Tales of Efflorescence

Once, I thought I could knit so fine,
With soft threads meant to croon,
But surprise! My scarf is a line,
That looks more like a curious broom.

That tangled mess, a tale unwound,
With petals sprouting from each seam,
The pigeons cheer, they're quite spellbound,
While my attempts, they fly like a dream.

Each loop a riddle, each twist a jest,
As flowers bloom from silly strife,
In every error, humor's best,
Finding joy in this knitting life.

So let's craft down this laughable path,
With colors bright, and nods to fate,
In the petals where chuckles can bathe,
A garden of giggles, we celebrate!

Ties That Hold Rather Than Bind

With knots as friends, we're never apart,
Instead, we gather as one grand team,
Tales of ties, a giggle-thirsty heart,
Where yarn loops become our dream.

Oh my, the fumbles, the stretchy woes,
Each clasp of laughter a silly bind,
Weaving stories like wild garden hose,
Chasing each other while being kind.

My scarf's a snake, a slithering foe,
Entangled by giggles, we have some fun,
These ties of humor, they endlessly grow,
With frayed edges shining under the sun.

So let's raise our hooks and give a cheer,
For ties that thread joy through every day,
With smiles binding us ever near,
In our silly, woven ballet!

Fragments of History in Weave

Once a table cloth was bold,
Now it drapes a tale untold.
Pasta stains from feasts we had,
Grandma's secrets, they're not bad.

Delicate patterns serve their fate,
As napkin ghosts we often hate.
In picnics, they've become our mates,
Discovering crumbs—what a state!

Every thread holds laughter's grace,
With tiny mishaps, they embrace.
From tea spills to crafty tricks,
A lace life we just can't fix.

So here's to fibers, wild and free,
Creating chaos, joy, and glee.
In the stitches, life's absurd,
Each tiny knot, a memory stirred.

Echoes of Joy in Each Loop

Thread by thread, we giggle along,
With every loop, we sing our song.
Sticky fingers, laughs galore,
Lace mishaps—who could want more?

Once a placemat, now a hat,
Fails so funny, we roll on that.
A game of hide and seek we'll play,
With lacey ghosts, we're here to stay.

Baked some cookies, oops, oh dear,
Crumbs and lace cloth make us cheer.
No dinner manners, just pure delight,
In this fabric, we take flight.

As we weave with joy so bright,
Memories twirl in every sight.
So let's embrace this tangled bliss,
With laughter in every twist and kiss.

Lace Dreams Beneath Stardust Skies

Under the moon, we dance with flair,
Wearing lace like we don't care.
A picnic blanket turns to dreams,
In silly tunes, we burst at seams.

Lace umbrellas keep the rain,
While neighbors grumble, full of disdain.
But beneath this white and twirls of glow,
We laugh so loud, they'll never know.

Butterflies in lace take flight,
As pockets fill with stars so bright.
With lace wings, we float away,
Chasing dreams till break of day.

So here's to whimsy, chaos, cheer,
In lacey dreams, we persevere.
A sprinkle of stardust on our shoes,
In this funny dance, we can't lose.

The Artistry of Fragility

With whispered winds, the laces sway,
Creating mischief in their play.
A fragile art that makes us grin,
Where laughter blooms, and fun begins.

An old armchair, covered with cheer,
Bound to crumble, but we hold dear.
Every tear tells a funny tale,
Of past shenanigans that prevail.

In the garden, lace does bloom,
A frail display that brightens gloom.
As butterflies land, we stifle giggles,
At teacup creatures and playful wiggles.

So here's to laughter, light and free,
In fragile art, we find the key.
With every snip and every tear,
Life's funny moments float in the air.

www.ingramcontent.com/pod-product-compliance
Lightning Source LLC
Chambersburg PA
CBHW070329120526
44590CB00017B/2840